How To Emigrate The Right Way

RAMON GUTIERREZ

DEDICATION

This book is dedicated to my wife and kids, which are my life companions in all of my escapades, with moving abroad being the most important and most exciting one of them all. Thank you for being my adventure buddies in this exciting movie we call life! I also dedicate it to each and every one of the millions of people who are, were or have ever been an immigrant. Becoming one can be a hard and difficult choice full of uncertainties and unknowns, as the people who embark on this road do it at the expense of leaving behind everything and everyone they know: their culture, their customs, their loved ones. But, if done right, it's also a road that is full of rewards, accomplishments, and a better future. As an immigrant myself, I want to tell you all, that I'm cheering for your success. Hang in there, keep plowing forward, and don't deviate from your plan and goals. If you do that, I can assure you'll eventually reach your objective, and it will all be worth it.

TABLE OF CONTENTS

ACKNOWLEDGMENTS

I'd like to express my deepest gratitude to all the people that supported me and provided me with their valuable help throughout this project. You all know who you are. Thank you very much.

PROLOGUE

Emigrating to new places is something very common, not only in this era, but throughout the history of humanity. The first human beings emigrated from the African continent to Europe and Asia, in a process lasting thousands of years, and which continued until they populated all the continents of the planet, including places as remote and difficult to reach as Oceania. The arrival of Europeans to the Americas was another example of massive emigration that led to the meeting of the natives and the immigrants, and which culminated in the Europeanization of the American continent, to the detriment of the existing indigenous population. The above examples show that emigration is a more than common event, and even something innate to the nature of mankind.

There are many reasons why someone decides to leave behind everything they know and emigrate to new lands, and each case is unique and different depending on each person, but usually this decision is summarized in one main motive that covers a wide spectrum of reasons: the search for a better quality of life and a more promising future for you and your loved ones. Basically, any reason for emigration can be circumscribed to this motive. At the same time, the search for a better quality of life can be focused on such key areas as the economy, family reunification, health, security, education, labour, among others. But it can also be focused on such mundane topics as the nightlife of a certain city, the available extracurricular activities, the attraction to a certain culture, etc.

Regardless of the reason, the important thing is to realize that emigration is a fairly important decision that affects the life of not only the person who emigrates, but also of the people around them, and therefore this decision should not be taken lightly, and it must be given all the importance and attention it deserves, always weighing in all the pros and cons of taking a path with such a high potential to alter our entire surroundings.

In my particular case, I decided to emigrate to Canada from the Dominican Republic, moved by different reasons, but, as I mentioned before, all of my reasons translated into one motive: the search for a better quality of life and a better future for me and my family. I will expand on my own experience in more detail throughout this book, not with the intention of influencing your decision making, but to use real life examples of how someone else did it, with the hope that this information will help others achieve a better life for them and their loved ones, whatever reasons to emigrate they have.

While this book is designed for the people that want to emigrate by following the legal emigration process and guidelines provided by the different countries around the world, and is not actually intended for the ones that can emigrate by other means (e.g. through marriage, descent, or by illegal ways), it still has valuable information that can be used by anyone looking for guidance on specific subjects that usually affect all emigrants no matter their method for moving abroad.

I really hope that you find value in my words, and that I am able to help at least a few of my fellow emigrants. If I can do that for even just one person, then this book will have fulfilled its purpose. Now, let's get started!

CHAPTER 1

Make a Decision

Deciding and committing to your decision will be the key for success on this endeavour, so make sure you take your time and think things through in a thorough way.

F irst things first. The most important part of this journey is making sure that you want to emigrate for real. I'm not talking about those spur of the moment situations that make you wish you lived elsewhere, or the ones that come to you after you watch a documentary or read a book about a certain country that makes your mind daydream about how it would be to live there. If those are the reasons why you are thinking about emigrating to a different country, I'd recommend you close this book and concentrate on improving your quality of life in the place that you currently call home. If you do have an important reason, then keep on reading.

Becoming an immigrant in a foreign land is a big, BIG decision, so if this is the road you want to take, it better be due to something meaningful and quite important. Remember, you will be leaving behind everything and everyone you know to start from scratch a new life in a different place. It doesn't necessarily mean that only the people who are politically or religiously persecuted in their homeland are the ones that should consider relocating somewhere else, but wanting to leave your country because you don't like the traffic in your city, or the taxes you pay, or the noisy neighbour you have, just won't cut it. You have to have a meaningful and strong enough reason that will keep you focused and on track at all times, and makes you follow the road map that you'll draw to achieve this goal without faltering or hesitating. For better understanding, I will explain the particular reasons why I decided to move abroad to a foreign land.

I was born in 1977 in the Dominican Republic, a small, idyllic tropical paradise half-island in the middle of the Caribbean, where I had a happy childhood full of fond memories, growing up in a close-knit and very loving middle-class family, which provided me with everything I needed, without excesses, but also without deficiencies. I remember my neighbourhood being very similar to those you see in the United States, with nice wide streets and beautiful houses with green gardens, kids playing in the street, and not a worry about anything. My father, a Civil Engineer, had a good job at an Engineering firm in the private sector, and was able to provide us with everything we needed, despite his income being the only one in the household, as my mother stayed home to take care of me and my two siblings. Back then, the total population of the country was around 5.4 million, there were plenty of opportunities and people who studied and became professionals had a good chance of finding a good job in their area that would allow them to provide for their family. Criminality was low, there was widespread respect for social order, and government corruption, while it existed, was not widespread and wasn't a big of an issue.

Fast forward 35 years, and the picture was quite different. The neighbourhood where I grew up looks now like a military camp, with the green gardens transformed into concrete fences with barbed wires on top, and the kids in the street have been swapped by car jams and gridlocks. The population has pretty much doubled, opportunities are very scarce, criminality is extremely high (hence the concrete fences and barbed wires), and government corruption is running rampant. By this time, I am a Civil Engineer, just like my father, but unlike him, I also have a Postgraduate degree in Construction Management, and speak fluent English, while my wife is an Architect, also bilingual. Despite having these attributes, along with all of our years of experience in our pertinent areas, me and my wife were struggling to make ends meet, while at the same time we saw that the people who thrived were the ones with government connections, instead of the ones with the necessary education and preparation. Corruption was rewarded, while integrity was mocked. We also saw how drug trafficking and the related criminality that comes with it, was swallowing the island whole, with the country becoming the main point of drug transfer from South America to the United States and Europe.

What my father was able to accomplish by himself with his own merits 30 years before me, was something that my wife and I were struggling to accomplish together, and with two small kids under our care, we could foresee how much more difficult it would be for our children to be successful 30 more years down the road. That, along with the very high criminality and the degradation of values in that society, is what prompted us to make the decision of leaving the place we called home, for a new place in the search for financial stability, moral values, and a better future for our kids.

So, as you can see, my reasons to leave were meaningful and strong, as the lack of opportunity, lack of security, and the need to search for a better future for my kids are very valid justifications.

They were solid enough to keep us on track throughout the duration of the process from the very idea inception, and all the way to even after we got to where we emigrated to. Having well-founded reasons like these is of extreme importance, as there will be many instances during your journey where you will find obstacles, will be discouraged by others, or will feel the need to quit, and the reasons that have prompted you to decide to emigrate will be the only thing that will stand between deciding to continue moving forward or giving up.

Once you've analyzed your particular situation and have come up with a set of good reasons to leave your country, I would advise you to write these down and keep them in a place of easy access where you can take a look at them anytime you feel the need to pull the plug on this endeavour. If they are compelling enough, they will reinforce the need for you to continue moving forward with your plan no matter what. Take your time while searching for your reasons, you shouldn't rush this brainstorming session. I will see you in the next chapter once you have them.

CHAPTER 2

Choose a Place to Start Your New Life

Selecting your new country is the most important decision you'll need to make on this journey, as you'll be choosing the place to spend the rest of your life, so you have to make sure you pick the right one.

W hen you are born, you don't have a say on where that happens. You are confined to where your parents reside, or decide to reside. Some people are lucky enough to have their parents, at their time of birth, located in a place where people can live happy, in peace, and with prosperity. But that is not the case for many others, where the only thing they can count on is on having roadblocks to achieving happiness and success.

Now, when you are an adult, you are no longer bound to be at the place where you were brought to this world. You can now make your own decisions and actually choose where you want to spend the rest of your life at. Think of it as being reborn, but, unlike the first time, you now get the chance to choose where to reborn.

This is a crucial step, as the place where you want to relocate to needs to be a place that you actually like, understand, and appreciate. If, for example, you base your decision only in the economics and end up choosing a place that you don't connect with (maybe you don't like the weather, or the culture, or have issues with the language), you might fulfill your dream of earning more money than at your previous country, but still feel miserable in all other aspects of your life, as everything that surrounds you will remind you of all the things that you actually dislike of your new homeland. Remember, this is a long term plan, so you have to make sure that you can absorb all the things that come with the country you choose, good and bad, and still be happy. Making a list of the countries that you feel connected to and where you would like to emigrate to, is the first step you'll need to take in this part of the process.

Second, you need to make sure that the place you pick is open to immigration and actually embraces having people from other cultures join them. You definitely don't want to move to a place where you will be discriminated against, or be treated as a second class citizen. The place you choose must be a place where you will be presented with the same opportunities as everybody else that lives on that society, and ideally even provides new immigrants with aid and support to help them during the early stages of their move, with the intention of increasing their chance of success.

Third, you have to be objective when making your selection, and use your logic and your common sense during this process, and let your feelings aside. There might be a few options for you to choose where to relocate to, but since moving abroad is such a drastic and radical change in your life, one that is full of risks, you want to ensure that you pick the place where you have the better chances at succeeding in your endeavour, even if it's not the place where your heart is aiming for. I do encourage you to have several options to choose from, so that you can make sure that the one you select is the best one that suits your needs, while also having a back-up destination in case the main one doesn't pan out for whatever reason, but always, and I mean always, be objective when choosing your pick.

Lastly, one other thing you need to take into account before selecting your destination is the related cost of the whole process, from the initial documents you need to get when you first start, to the final fees you'll need to pay once your application is approved. No matter which place you pick, you will have to spend money in order to get your application completed and submitted, so you should make sure that you are financially apt to see this process through. The costs will vary depending on the country of your choosing, so you should make sure that your finances are sound enough for you to face all of the associated costs, and that spending this money won't affect your role as a provider to your family. I wouldn't go as far as saying that you should choose based solely on these costs, as the main driver should be knowing you have the better chances of success, as previously mentioned, but you should definitively take these costs into account when making a decision, as depending on your particular situation, the costs of a specific place could be prohibitive, on which case you should then aim for the second pick. Now, let's take a look at my case.

When I was on this step, me and my family had 4 options to choose from: United States, Canada, Australia, and Spain. We had some savings set aside for this, and after quickly investigating about the costs of legally emigrating to each of them, we realized money would not be an issue for us with regards to applying to any of these 4 places, so we moved on to consider other sets of parameters.

Of the four potential destinations we could pick from, we had only visited one, the US. With Dominican Republic being practically the backyard of the US, it seemed like the logical option to choose that country, as we would be closer to the family and friends we were leaving behind, plus we knew many people in the States. Ironically, this was the first country we scratched off from our list, as the roads available for us to immigrate there were the most difficult of all four, and the path to citizenship was even harder.

The next one on our list to be dropped was Australia. Their immigration path was less complicated than the one from the US, but still, it wasn't something that we could control, as we would have to apply and wait to see if the Australian government eventually invited us to continue with our application, which could take years. Also, the fact that Australia was so far away from our country of birth, meant that all the people we were leaving behind would hardly ever visit us, and for us to go back to visit them would turn out to be extremely costly. Due to that, Australia was dismissed.

Then, there were Canada and Spain. Between the two, I was originally more inclined towards Spain, while my wife was more inclined towards Canada. In the case of Spain, being from a Latin-American country, we already had the language, and the culture was similar. Since my father is a Spaniard, I had it pretty easy to get Permanent Resident status just by requesting it once I arrived to Spain, which meant that we had total control of the immigration path. So far, so good. I also had a brother in Spain, so moving there meant that we would be with family. Since it all seemed to be aligning with Spain, I then decided to do a solo recon trip to the old continent and visit the motherland, to see how it looked like, and get a feel of how life might be there.

I'm really happy I did that recon trip, for as much of a great country that Spain is – a place full of history and wonderful things to see, interesting and fascinating in so many different ways – it actually turned out to be not that attractive to me, at least not for relocating there permanently. I found it to be very crowded for my liking, with people living in tiny yet very expensive apartments, and it looked very old for my taste. I didn't scratch it from my list yet, but the fact that I didn't find it as appealing as I thought, prompted me to turn my attention to the last option we had left: Canada.

We had never been to Canada either, but we had been to the US, and we knew, based on reading, that Canada and the US were similar in many ways, like having plenty of green open spaces all over the place, extended and spacious cities, big and more affordable housing, and a more modern architecture, all of which are things that we like. Due to that, we decided there was no need to take a recon trip there. We then started investigating about Canada's immigration program, and saw that they had a program reserved for skilled workers, and on their list of desired professions, mine was on the list. Digging a bit more, we learned that their immigration program was based on points, and as long as you got the minimum number of points needed, and as long as the quota wasn't filled by the time your file was reviewed and processed at the pertinent immigration office, you would be approved and given a Permanent Resident visa. This meant that we could have control of our immigration path, as long as we met the minimum threshold stipulated by Canada.

The next step we took was to determine if based on several factors which included, among other things, our age, professional experience, and language proficiency, we would meet the minimum threshold. Our age and professional experiences were easy to confirm as a good fit for the program, but for our language proficiency we needed to take a test recognized by Immigration Canada to confirm our level of proficiency for the English language, and in the Dominican Republic that test had a cost of US$425 per person, a significant amount of money for us since my wife earned just a few dollars above that figure per month at her job as an Architect! In our specific case, since I was going to be the main applicant, as long as I aced the test, there wasn't a need for my wife to take it herself. Since we were already decided about moving abroad (as per the first step outlined on this book), we didn't hesitate and proceeded to pay for my test, even with the uncertainty of whether or not I would get a good enough of a grade that would allow us to meet the minimum threshold. It was a risk, but it was a risk we accepted since we had made up our minds about moving abroad, and we didn't think twice when the time came for us to take that gamble. I'm happy to say that our gamble paid off, and I got extremely good grades, which meant that we could proceed with moving forward with our plan.

Knowing by this time that we had two places where to choose from, we then were left with the task of choosing which one to put all of our attention and efforts towards to. To make that decision, we made a list of all the pros and cons of each place, and decided to give a bigger weight to the pros that meant having a higher chance of success once we emigrated. To make the story short, Canada and Spain each had their share of good things, as well as bad, but there were two reasons that prompted us to make our final decision. The first one was the fact that during that period of time, which was just a few years after the big housing bubble that caused the world's markets to crash in 2008, Spain's unemployment rate was off the charts, in the double digits, which meant we would be facing very high competition in order to get a job, especially as immigrants, while at the same time salaries were very low. Canada, on the other hand, had an unemployment rate in the low single digits, and salaries were very competitive. The second reason was that with Canada being an immigrant dependent country, they had a very well set up immigration system, designed to attract qualified professionals while helping them settle in once they arrived, and become productive members of their society as quick as possible, something Spain was completely lacking. Since it was the logical decision to choose the place where we would have the bigger chances of getting a well-paying job fast, while also providing us the right tools to become part of that new society, Canada was the obvious winner. So, we chose

Canada, and drifted our attention to that country and their immigration policy and requirements.

As you can see, even with the fact that we had family at one of our potential destinations while at the same time it also matched our language and culture, it still did not make it our final pick, as we were pretty objective in our choosing, and instead of picking with our hearts, we decided to select the place where we knew we would have the better chances of success. As previously said, moving abroad is a big risk, and when taking a risk, you have to use your brains without letting your feelings get in the way. If you let them get in the way, you risk making the wrong decision, one that you might end up regretting.

CHAPTER 3

Do Your Own Homework

When planning to move abroad, there's a lot of information that you need to gather, study and analyze in order to make the right decisions. The task of finding and digesting all this data is for you, and only you to do.

B y this time, you've now decided you want to emigrate, and you've chosen a place to emigrate to. That is great, but having made those two decisions are just the initial actions on a long list of steps. Now it's the time for you to get your hands dirty, do your homework and actually find out what are the things you need to be able to successfully submit your application. The main thing to acknowledge at this stage is that this homework needs to be done in a thorough way by yourself, not someone else. You might be thinking "Duh, of course it will be done by me, who else would be doing it?", and that is a fair (yet snarky) response, but you would be surprised to know how many people I've seen relying on others to do their dirty work for them during this step. Remember, you are the one who wants to emigrate, and as the person with a real interest on achieving this goal, you are the only one that can really put all the effort needed to make this a reality. As much as others tell you they can do it for you, or help you with some of the tasks, experience tells me the chances of this turning into anything of real value are slim, and you run the risk of missing key input by not submerging yourself into the vast pool of information available for this.

With the above statement I'm not saying that you can't or shouldn't use the help of others, or the services of a lawyer that is well versed on immigration matters that pertain to the country of your choosing, as it is perfectly fine to reach for help, and sometimes it might be a must. But what I'm saying is that even if you decide to use that help, you should still do your own homework by yourself, parallel to them, as if you didn't have anyone else helping you, as no matter how much knowledge on the subject the people helping you have, they could still miss something important that could affect whether or not you get your application approved. Immigration policies are constantly changing, and it is very hard to keep up with them. A policy or requirement in place today, might not be in place tomorrow, so by you investigating from your end, you can make sure that you have the latest data about this process, while also making sure that the ones helping you are not jumping any steps or using outdated info. One important thing to keep in mind here is that, depending on the place you chose to emigrate to, chances are that their immigration policies are quite clear and you can find online all the information you need about that. If it's an immigration prone country, I would be surprised if their steps and requirements are not exposed crystal clear on their pertinent immigration website.

You should also know that in many countries you can do all the paperwork and submit it yourself without the need for a lawyer or representative, if that is the route you wish to take. On the other hand, if you decide to use the services of a lawyer, please investigate very thoroughly about the ones you intend to use, and make sure that they are approved to do this work on your behalf and have good reviews. There are many great lawyers out there, but there are also a lot of scammers that present themselves as lawyers when they really aren't, and the second you pay them, the second they disappear. Again, do your homework, read, investigate, ask a lot of questions, and make sure you feel 100% comfortable with the person of your choosing before handing them any money.

In my case, Canada has an excellent and very detailed immigration website called Citizenship and Immigration Canada (CIC) that has all the answers that you could possibly need. At the beginning, me and my wife were prone to use a well-known lawyer that has experience with Canadian immigration, but after surfing and reading through the CIC website, we realized that there wasn't a need for us to spend that money as long as we followed their stipulated guidelines. Most of the steps that needed to be taken would have to be done by us anyways even if we used a lawyer, so it didn't make sense for us to spend extra money on those services if we were the ones doing most of the leg work. With that decision made, we then prepared a list of all the requirements, rolled up our sleeves, and got to work.

We concentrated first on making sure we were able to acquire every single document being requested by the CIC, as if there was even one that we couldn't produce, then the whole application would fail. Luckily for us, we confirmed that everything that was to be submitted, we could get. There were police certificates, birth and marriage certificates, bank letters, professional certificates, university transcripts, sworn affidavits, etc, etc, etc… and etc again. It was a big pile of documents, all of which cost money to get, and all of which had to be translated from Spanish to English by a certified translator, which also cost money. As stated in the previous chapter, this is one of the things you need to keep in mind, you will spend a lot of money to get your application completed, so you should make sure that you have the financial capacity to see this process through.

At the same time that we were gathering all the needed documentation, we started searching online for advice from others that had recently done the same, just to make sure we were filling up the paperwork the right way. We joined online forums and WhatsApp groups where there were people that were emigrating or had recently emigrated to Canada, and we asked questions and read the different posts made by others related to the inquiries we had. Please note the word "recently" that I've already used a couple of times. I've used this word not by mere chance, but on purpose, as per my previous comments, immigration requirements vary with frequency, so a year-old post might already be outdated as the steps or requirements might have changed and be different today.

You also need to keep in mind that you shouldn't blindly rely on online groups or social media, as these are full of garbage information and ill advice from people that don't have a clue of what they are doing but that act like if they were eminences on the matter, so you need to filter these down very thoroughly by investigating and comparing with government provided documentation. But, if used correctly, these can also be a source of helpful advice.

From that huge pile of information, we picked and chose what we considered of value, and disposed of the rest. We then corroborated that information with the one available at the CIC, just to make sure it was accurate or that it didn't contradict any of their processes. When we had a doubt that could not be answered or clarified by anyone, we used our common sense, and went down the safe path by exceeding the expectations. When you are uncertain of something, it's always best to over deliver than to under deliver.

The process of acquiring all the needed documentation is quite extensive, as there are many documents that need to be government certified, so you have to wait for the pertinent institutions to issue them and then send them to the corresponding government offices for certification.

In our case, that would take several weeks at best, and there were documents that were dependent on other documents, so you had to wait to get some of them issued before you could proceed and request others, so while we were waiting for some of the documentation, we were also organizing ourselves and drawing up a plan, a step that I will expand in the next chapter. I will see you there!

CHAPTER 4

Organize Yourself and Draw Up a Plan

As with any major project, you need to draw up a plan that guides you through the whole process of emigrating from beginning to end, as this will help you stay on track following the logical order of things.

A s a project manager myself, I can tell you that whenever you have a project, no matter the size of it, you will need to break it down into activities, organize it and create a plan that shows you which activities go first, and which activities follow afterwards. Well, you can be sure that moving abroad is indeed a project, and not a small one. There are so many things that you need to do when you are embarking in an endeavour like this, that you need to have a roadmap of what to do and when to do it, otherwise you run the risk of getting sidetracked or overwhelmed, while also being prone to making mistakes or missing steps or deadlines. So, for you to know where to focus your attention, you need to organize yourself and draw up a plan that you can follow step by step. This will allow you to stay focused, keep in line with your goals, and to concentrate on the right activities and tasks. You should also decide on a departure date goal to hop on a plane and start your new life in a new country, as this will allow you to prepare a schedule that can fit your timeline.

Going back to my experience, once my wife and I knew that we met all the CIC requirements and that we could prepare a full application package for submission, besides getting started with acquiring all the necessary documentation, we also began learning about Canada, its climate, its culture, its different provinces and cities, access to education, access to healthcare, quality of life, job opportunities, and cost of living, among others. We wanted to understand where in Canada we could have the best quality of life that would fit our needs, besides having enough opportunities for us to have success professionally. Since my wife has a rare medical condition, we also had to make sure that the place we chose had access to the specialists she required. On top of that, because we had two small children, it was also important for us to know beforehand how the school system worked, how to enroll them, and which schools were the better ones for them to attend. For that, we had to select a province, a city, and even a neighbourhood.

Since we had a departure date goal that we wanted to meet, all of our tasks needed to be completed by certain dates (you don't have to be accurate down to specific days, depending on how much time in advance of your planned departure date you start, your scheduled completion dates can be a range of several weeks or even months), so as you can see, we were juggling a lot of different moving parts to this process, and without a plan in place, you can just imagine how close to impossible it would have been for us to know what to do and on which order, so I'm guessing that by now you can appreciate how important this step is.

This is when my wife's awesome organizational skills came into place. While I was doing the tedious and hard work of acquiring all the documents we needed, she drafted a plan outlining each step that needed to be completed for us to achieve all milestones and, ultimately, our end goal. I won't include the plan we (she) prepared, as each case will be different and unique, but I can give you a small example of a few of the main things that we included in our roadmap for you to have an idea of what you may need to include in yours (remember, all the below mentioned activities happened at the same time we were gathering our documents to be submitted):

- Search for the best places to live in your new country.
- Investigate about the job market in those areas.
- Investigate about the healthcare system in those areas.
- Investigate about the school system in those areas.
- Investigate about housing.
- Investigate about the cost of living.
- Find out which additional documents you will need once you arrive (e.g. for validating your driver's license, for enrolling the kids in school, etc.).
- Put a price to all your personal belongings.
- Start looking for potential buyers for your personal belongings.
- Investigate about disenrolling from all public and government institutions at your country of origin (e.g. tax office, social security, electrical service, etc.).

The above list is just a fraction of all the things we had in ours, but it can give you a pretty good idea of what it looked like and can drive you in the right direction when creating yours. We also included milestone dates for when we would aim to have each document ready for submission and added a tentative final submission date. On top of that, we allowed for a few months for getting a response back from the CIC office, getting our medicals done, and getting the final Permanent Resident visa issued. This gave us a tentative date of when we could probably expect to have in our hands all the documentation that we needed to leave. With that tentative date, we then added some extra time for how long we thought it could take us to get our things in order prior of leaving, selling all of our stuff, and finding a place where to stay in Canada once we arrived there. Pretty intense, right? Not really, it sounds more complicated than it actually is. Once you sit down and draft your plan, as long as it is logical, detailed and in proper order, you'll start to see that things will begin to fall into place, so don't be discouraged by the amount of work to be done at this stage.

It's also good to note that there are many things on your list that you can't really control (e.g. the time that the immigration office will take reviewing your case, or whether or not you'll need additional medical tests), these dates are not set in stone, they are just preliminary and will most likely need to be adapted and modified as you go, but even so, having a preliminary schedule will be of extreme help in getting you in the correct track.

After we had our plan put together (list of tasks and schedule), we then got submerged on anything that had to do with Canada as a country, as well as with their immigration system. It was our day-to-day task whenever we were not working or taking care of the kids. We devoted ourselves to learning everything we needed to learn in order for us to find all the answers to our questions, and to be able to make an educated decision based on facts that checked all boxes.

Once we completed one of the activities, we then jumped to the following one, always in order, never jumping the line, as doing so would defeat the whole purpose of organizing ourselves. We took notes about the things we learned and used those notes to decide which way to go. Doing it like this allowed us to take every step and make every decision with certainty, while at the same time it helped us keep up with our schedule, and at the end of the process it really made a difference, as once we were about to leave, we were confident enough that we had all bases covered and there weren't any uncertainties. By the time we hoped on our plane, we didn't have any second thoughts, doubts or fear. Instead, we felt happy and completely secure of what we were doing. Hopefully, this will be your case too!

CHAPTER 5

Avoid Escape Clauses

Escape clauses are the biggest threats of this whole process, as they are tailored solely for self-sabotaging purposes. As such, if you want to have a chance of succeeding on this project, you should refrain from implementing them at all costs.

When you decide to emigrate, you are making a very important decision, so if you really want to be successful at achieving that goal, then you need to be all the way into that undertaking and be 100% sure of your objective and of the desire and willingness to reach it. If you have doubts or think you will not put all the effort and attention that is needed on this task, then you have a good chance of not following through until the end. This could be as simple as just flatly giving up on it halfway through, but it can also be done by the use of what I call escape clauses. Before I go and explain what escape clauses are, I need to first define what, in my eyes, are the 3 different types of people that make up our society.

There are people in this world that know what they want, they go for it and never stop until they acquire it. I call these people the "Go-getters". There are others that know what they want, and they give it a shot with the hope to achieve that goal, but if things get difficult, then they just bail. This type of people want someone else to do the dirty work for them. I call these the "Lazies". And then there are the ones who like to lie to themselves thinking that they know what they want, when what they really want is actually the opposite. I call these the "Dreamers". You might be thinking that this last group of people is just the odd ball and that there aren't many like this. Well, I haven't done a scientific trial to come up with numbers on this, but after hearing many, many people that have come to me for advice on how to emigrate, I can tell you with confidence that the people that make up this group are far more than what you think. In fact, I can honestly say most of the people that approach me for advice on how to achieve what I achieved, are in this group.

The individuals that comprise the first group, the Go-getters, will succeed reaching their end goal, as long as they qualify to meet all necessary requirements. The ones in the middle group, the Lazies, have a much lower chance of success, as when things get too complicated (which most likely will happen with something as challenging as emigrating), they will just give up, unless, of course, they have someone else to do all the dirty work for them. The people that make up the last group, the Dreamers, those are bound to fail, not because they don't have the ability to get it done, but because they secretly don't want to succeed, and the only reason they give it a shot is their need to make themselves and others believe that they tried, when in reality their decision not to be successful on this endeavour was made even before starting.

For you to have any chance of succeeding on reaching your emigration goal, you need to be part of the Go-getters. If you are not part of that group, then my advice for you is to not waste any time and money on this and concentrate your efforts on something else.

"And how do I know which group I'm part of?", you may ask. Well, I believe that if you are asking yourself that question, chances are that you are not a Go-getter. Still, let's say you believe you are truly ready to do what it takes to get to the finish line on this project, but at the same time you are still a bit dubious of how you will react when you start facing obstacles, and want to try to figure out beforehand whether or not you will end up quitting or sabotaging yourself. In this case, based on my experience I can share with you a few of the signs I've noticed on people that belong on the Lazies and on the Dreamers.

With the Lazies, the first sign that they show is that they get overwhelmed from the get go, and don't want to put even the minimum effort into reading and digesting the information that is available for them in order to know what steps to take. They want someone else to digest that information for them and feed it to them like birds do with their hatchlings. Every time they complete a step, if the next one is a difficult one, they whine and complain, and start procrastinating and looking for excuses not to do it. Most of the time, when the Lazies jump into an ambitious venture, they do it along with other people who have the same goal, with the intention of leaning on them (leaching off of them) when they come in front of a hard obstacle and avoid getting greasy hands themselves. They will only be able to reach their target as long as they have a Go-getter as part of their group, hence why the vast majority of the Lazies give up sometime during the length of the process.

The Dreamers, on the other hand, have no interest at all in reaching their goal, so they won't leach off anybody. They will just create a bunch of escape clauses that will ultimately lead to them ditching their plans with a "justified excuse", one that will make them believe that the reason they were not able to succeed was out of their hands, while also making them feel that they did all they could to reach their target, when in reality, they didn't.

So, after a lengthy go-around explaining the different types of people, their way of thinking, and their modus operandi, we finally got to the part where I explain what escape clauses are, although by now I'm pretty sure you must have a pretty good idea of what they are. As implied on the previous paragraph, escape clauses are situations that some people meticulously and deliberately put themselves into, knowing that by doing that, they are effectively torpedoing themselves out of the game. These escape clauses are never random things that happen, they are very well thought out and planned, and the people who use them know that these will prevent them from reaching what they want to make themselves and others believe are their goals.

The strange thing is, that even though these are calculated events, most people are not aware that they are using escape clauses, in fact, they don't even know these exist, and they truly believe that they are doing what it takes to achieve the very same goal that, in reality, they are torpedoing. The reasons for this odd behaviour are well above the capabilities of this book, as to better understand the root cause of this conduct, it would entail a more in-depth analysis by a professional in the field of human psychology, which I am not, but the point is that this type of self-sabotage happens, and it happens more often than not. My personal opinion is that this type of people do this because, while deep in their hearts they know what's best for them, they are too afraid of taking a risk, and since they don't want to feel that they missed on a specific opportunity due to lack of action, they get started on trying to seize that opportunity, making themselves believe that they are giving it a chance and doing everything they can to accomplish their goal, but along the way they unconsciously (and sometimes consciously) set unattainable objectives, or put themselves in dead end paths or roads that lead to failure, which will eventually prevent them from achieving their end target.

A good example of these escape clauses is when people use the services of a lawyer for emigrating purposes, but put no effort at all into trying to find the best paths by themselves and completely rely on the lawyer's will, resolution and capacity to decide for them the best option or path to take. Not to speak ill of lawyers, as many of them do an outstanding job, but at the end of the day, the lawyer gets paid either way, whether you get approved to emigrate or not, maybe not the complete fee but a big chunk of it for sure, so some of them will not put the same effort that you, the interested party, would. A lot of Dreamers know this, based on their specific situation, whether it is their advanced age in relation to a specific Country's age requirement, or their language skills, so they choose to hire a lawyer to decide for them and wash their hands of the outcome, knowing ahead of time that their chances of success are slim at best. Lawyers are professionals, but only you know your specific needs, weaknesses and strengths, so there's nothing wrong with you steering your lawyer in the direction that you believe is of your best convenience. If you leave it all to them without putting any effort from your end, you are effectively a Dreamer, hoping to fail.

Take a look at this other example. In the case of Canada, age is a big issue for emigrating purposes. As based on their latest requirements to get invited to apply as a Federal Skilled Worker under the Express Entry program, you start getting points deducted once you turn 30 years old, which is still quite young. Some people that have approached me for advice are either on their late 30's or early to mid 40's, which means that the chances of them being invited are close to none, unless they have an out of this world education and professional résumé, which in the situations that I'm referring to, was not the case. The only way this type of people have a chance is by coming to Canada to study for one or two years, then applying for a work visa, and then after a few more years, applying to Permanent Residency, which is a more difficult and costly path than if you arrive through the Express Entry with a Permanent Residency from the get go. If you really know what you want and what's best for you, and have set your goals and made up your mind about achieving them, you will not hesitate while going through the more difficult and lengthy path that has better chances of success, as you know that the rewards will eventually dwarf the sacrifices, rather than continuing on the less difficult road, deep down knowing you will not be invited to apply, ever. Despite of this, some of the people that I'm referring to chose the latter, and their excuse was that they couldn't force destiny, and that if it was in their cards to get invited, they would be, no matter the road they took. That, in my books, is a perfect Dreamer specimen.

By this time hopefully you already know the difference between the Go-getters, the Lazies, and the Dreamers, while you should also be an expert at what escape clauses are. Defining which group you belong to will help you save time and money, as depending on the group you fall into, you can decide whether or not it makes sense to spend any resources on this endeavour. The idea is not to label people into any group, but to help you discover which group you belong to, and depending on which one it is, allow you to make the best decision for you and your loved ones.

CHAPTER 6

Be Discreet

Discretion will be one of your best allies during the initial stages of this venture, as it will help avoid unwanted noise and distraction from others, and allow you to concentrate on what you really need to focus.

By this point, if you are following through each of the steps outlined in this book, you should be on track to reaching your finish line. You now have decided that you want to emigrate, you've chosen a country were to emigrate to, you've made sure that you meet all minimum requirements to be accepted as an applicant, you've prepared your roadmap, started working on acquiring the pertinent paperwork, and are in the process of studying everything related to what will someday wishfully become your new country, learning about its history, its geography, its culture, and even making a list of potential cities to move to. Hopefully, you've also determined that you are on the Go-getters' group, which means that you are on a good path.

Now, as with any major change in life, at some point during this project's life cycle you will have to make everyone close to you aware about your intentions of moving abroad, and after that point, you will need to keep them posted on any status update regarding your application. Since we are dealing with such a major life changing event, it is just common sense and decency to keep your loved ones and everybody that matters to you in the loop with regards to any important new developments pertaining to this undertaking.

However, you don't want to rush into breaking this news at the early stages of the project, as depending on the case, you might end up getting a lot of resistance from your family and friends against the road that you want to take. Since nobody wants to see the people they care about leave to a faraway place, instead of showing support and understanding from the get go, their kneejerk reaction could be to try to demotivate you from continuing on that path, and you don't want that. The amount of stress that people that want to move abroad are exposed to is sometimes very high, just by the mere knowledge of the fact that, if accepted, they will be leaving behind everyone they know and will be headed into the unknown, so just imagine how much more difficult it would be for you by adding the extra stress of a disgruntled family, friend or group of friends telling you that what you are doing is crazy, selfish, unnecessary, risky, and many other negative connotations. Now, they don't do this to be mean-spirited, so you shouldn't take this type of reaction the wrong way. They do it because they love you and don't want to see you go. But the fact of the matter is that in this case, this reaction, even though it is based out of love, is bad for you, as it will bring you down, add stress, dampen your focus, undermine your determination, and overall make your goal a lot more difficult to reach.

During the early stages of this project, you don't need this. You don't need this at all. What you need is to be able to concentrate on your tasks in order to successfully complete them.

Due to this, it may be best for you to do all your preliminary investigation discreetly, and continue this way for as long as possible, at least until you are 100% sure that you meet all the requirements that you need in order to be approved for immigration purposes at the country of your choosing, and ideally until you have a solid plan properly set up and have a more clear idea of a tentative schedule that shows your timeline for leaving. Once you are at that stage, it is more difficult for the negative reactions or comments that could come from your family and friends to affect you or make you lose focus once they are made aware of your intentions of leaving. Every case is different, and in some situations discretion might not be needed, but if you believe your circumstances call for it, then follow this advice.

You could start testing the waters by feeding your close ones with limited information well ahead of breaking the news to them, ideally in a way that could be used as a preparation to what will eventually come. Things like randomly putting the subject of all the things that you dislike about the country where you live at, or the things that you dream of trying but aren't able to do at your current location, or comments about your professional future, or about raising a family, your eventual retirement, job uncertainty, education, etc. Depending on where you live, there are tons of topics that you could use to start rolling the ball indirectly, and the more often you do that, the lesser of a surprise it will be for them when you finally inform everybody about your plans. Many times, these same conversations will slowly lead to comments from others stating the positive side of starting a new life somewhere else, and that just works on your behalf. By slowly showing your family and friends all the things that you could gain by living abroad, at least some of them will eventually come to realize on their own terms that maybe moving abroad is not such a bad idea and that it could be the best way for you to achieve your dreams or to have a better life.

Once you've sufficiently marinated their minds with those types of subjects, you can then start telling a few of them (the closest and more open minded of your circle) about your will to start investigating a little bit about how to move abroad, just for general knowledge (never mind that you've already been investigating the crap out of this for the last 6 months!). This will show them that emigrating is not just something you like to talk about, but something that you are actually giving some serious thought to. After that, you can then update them every now and then with "new" info that you've "just found out" (wink-wink) about that process, and by doing that you will maintain their interest in the subject, and little by little start opening their minds about the fact that emigrating is a real possibility.

Eventually, once they've heard you talk so much about how living abroad would be a good thing in many cases, they will come to realize how much interest you really have on that field, and start accepting, even if unconsciously, that it really is a potential possibility that they should begin to acknowledge. At that moment, you will have a much easier and accepting crowd to eventually break the news to. Once they are at that stage, you should still proceed with caution and gentleness, and instead of flatly revealing your real plan to them, you should proceed to do it in stages, first telling them that you are seriously considering moving abroad due to such and such reasons, that you aren't decided, but that it is a real possibility to consider. With that groundwork done, you can then eventually tell them that you will start an application to the country of your choosing, just to see if you are able to meet the requirements (something you've probably done a long time ago by this time!), and from there on you can little by little get them up to date to where you're really at.

This method is not bullet proof, won't spare you negative reactions and won't prevent having people trying to get you stop thinking about moving abroad, but it will most certainly help dilute the news to them, while giving you the time to continue advancing in your project without unneeded distractions or major pushbacks. Because the timelines of migratory processes are usually long, you should have enough time to gradually feed all the pertinent information to the people you want to keep in the loop. By the time you are approved to move to your new country, your loved ones will already be aware of everything, and while some of them might still not agree that you are making the right decision, they will most likely have made peace with that reality and will hopefully support you in any way they can.

CHAPTER 7

Believe in Your Plan

One of the cornerstones of being successful on this journey is to be confident in your plan and believe in yourself and in the decisions you've made.

Have you ever made a decision, and right after started doubting yourself and having second thoughts about that very same decision you just made? Welcome to my world, which is also the world of 99.9% of people on this planet! I'm not a psychologist, but I believe it is engrained in human nature to reconsider most decisions they make, if not all. So, if (when) you find yourself second guessing your determination for moving abroad, don't be surprised or discouraged, as that's perfectly normal, especially with something as life changing as this.

Nevertheless, the mind can be very powerful, and if you don't have enough will power, that doubt can grow into an unmanageable monster that could put your whole plan in jeopardy by self-sabotage. That's why, for people to try to mitigate that risk, I've recommended throughout this book a series of steps to be followed, each of them with their own specific role in order to help avoid this monster to grow. Since you've already made an educated decision to emigrate based on a meaningful and strong reason or set of reasons, have done your preliminary homework and have prepared a sound and well-thought-out plan, then the only thing you need to do in order to appease this monster is to be confident and believe in your plan.

You need to keep focus and always move forward, never looking back. I can assure you that if you get to the finish line by following through each and every one of the steps outlined on this book, chances are that the rewards will be enormous and will outshine any downturns or potential risks you might foresee. You just need to believe that the plan that you've carefully crafted and meticulously developed will work, no matter how difficult the path to achieve it becomes, or how cloudy or muddy the road ahead looks.

There will be many instances throughout this journey where you will have to face enormous roadblocks and difficult barriers, and the only thing you can do about this is accept the fact that encountering these is inevitable. Have an open mind and be prepared to react in a positive yet assertive way when they happen, and continue plowing ahead one obstacle at a time. The last phrase is very important: "one obstacle at a time". On such a complex endeavour as the one you've embarked yourself on when deciding to emigrate, there are many moving parts that could get derailed when facing an obstacle, sometimes creating multiple obstacles at the same time, and when that happens, the best way to deal with these is to keep yourself composed, step back for a second, analyze the situation, and then make a decision.

Once you've evaluated the issues you've encountered, you should pick one to tackle first, choosing the one that makes more sense to deal with initially, not because it's the easiest one to resolve, but because it is the most important one. By important, I don't mean the level of difficulty to overcome, I mean the one that will open you the most doors. Let's suppose that at some point during your project's life cycle, you find yourself with 3 different issues at once that you need to resolve: issue A, issue B, and issue C. Issue A is a big one, so big that it is risking the whole project to fail if not resolved, but it will take a lot of time and effort to overcome. Issue B is not such a threat to the project, but without solving issue B, you can't get rid of issue A. Issue C is a minor issue that can be easily resolved at any time without the risk of majorly impacting the project.

On the above scenario, it stands to reason that the first issue to deal with would be issue B, as without that one out of the way, you can't fix issue A. Once issue B is out of the picture, you then should focus all of your energy into resolving issue A, as that one is risking the whole project to fail. Lastly, once you've gotten rid of issue A, you can then turn your attention to issue C, which is a simple one that does not have a major effect in the overall project. Since issue C is such an easy one to tackle, you might think why not deal with that one at the same time as either issue A or issue B to save yourself some time. My answer to that is yes, you could, but I wouldn't recommend it. When you put your attention in two different places at the same time, you are not putting your full focus at either one of them, you are distributing it, and while in many cases that wouldn't be a problem, there are instances where you need to devote all of your resources to just one place, or else you risk missing something that could hurt your project as a whole.

Since applying for emigration purposes should not be a race against the clock, then I don't see the point of risking missing any potential crucial step by trying to expedite your schedule by solving several issues together. The other problem I see with attending many issues at once is that you risk getting overwhelmed, and when that happens, you lose focus and mistakes are prone to be made. In extreme instances you could also get so frustrated and blocked that you might end up quitting the whole project. So, why risk it?

With that said, if you are facing a looming deadline that you need to meet for any specific reason, and resolving several issues at once is the only way you will have a chance of meeting that deadline, then by all means, multitask and solve away, but if that's not really your case, then I would advise for you to take your time doing things one step at a time, and not risk making mistakes or getting overwhelmed.

The important takeaway from all of this is that if you trust that the work you've done has been executed in a proper and thorough way, then you should have confidence in your plan without second thoughts and deviations. Believing in it is the best chance you have to succeed on this mission.

CHAPTER 8

Plan Ahead and Be Prepared

Being ahead of the game is a must when you are trying to start a new life abroad. Emigrating with unknowns, unanswered questions or with undetermined queries may translate into unwanted surprises for which you don't have a contingency plan for.

S o, you've managed to do all of your homework and all the legwork needed for this process and by now you consider yourself an expert in the realms of emigration to the country of your choosing. You've also acquired all needed documentation and have prepared a full application file that you believe meets all requirements requested by the immigration authority that you will be dealing with. You have even gone as far as submitting your application to the pertinent foreign government office, and are now waiting for them to get back to you with a response, one that you are hopeful but also extremely confident will be positive. Now what?

I'm pretty sure you wish my answer was for you to take a break, sit back and pamper yourself for doing such a great job. Well, I'm sorry to say it, but by now I believe you should already know that life is not that easy, at least not for the ones that want to be prepared ahead of time for what's to come. Now that you have completed all the hard work required to submit a proper application file and have found yourself with a lot of time back in your hands, it's moment for you to use that time to prepare a plan with all the steps you'll take once you arrive to your new country.

You definitely don't want to just hop on a plane and arrive to a place where you most likely don't know anyone and are not familiar with the culture, language and climate, just to start figuring things out at that moment. What you want is to have a well-thought-out plan that will guide you through the first weeks and months of stay at your new country, delineating all the steps to be taken, and the order in which to take them.

Let's once again put my experience as an example. Once my wife and I had submitted our application, we knew it would take several months for us to get a response, and instead of taking a break, we started making decisions of what our life would be like once we arrived. First thing we did was to decide which Canadian province and city within that province we would like to live at. Selecting the place to live at within the country of your choosing must be your first step to figure out, as most decisions (if not all) will depend on where you settle. Since Canada is such a large country, we had a really big map to select from, so we decided to be pragmatic about our decision making. We made a list of all provinces and territories that comprise the Canadian federation (thirteen in total) and started to scratch the ones that we knew we wouldn't want to live at based on our particular situation. Since we didn't like remote places and wanted to live in a big city with lots of opportunities, right from the get go we scratched from the list all three territories, which are further to the north. There was no point on entertaining the possibility of relocating in one of those places if we already knew that they were too remote for our liking. We then took a look at the remaining ten lower provinces. Since all of these had big enough cities, all ten of them could be the lucky winners to become our new home, so we then started to apply other filters.

For example, the first one to drop from the list of remaining provinces was Quebec. Quebec is a great province, with big vibrant cities, lots of culture and interesting places, while also full of opportunities, but it had one issue for us, and that was the language. As much as Canada is a bilingual society which by law states that you should have the same opportunities in both English and French, the reality is that French is the main language spoken in Quebec, and as such, being that we didn't know any French at all, we would struggle too much if we moved there. For us to be successful in that province, we would have to learn French, and that is not something you learn in a few days of study. Moving to Quebec would mean that we would be at a disadvantage compared to many other job seekers that speak French fluently, and since our goal was to get a good job as fast as possible, we knew that wouldn't be achievable in that province, so we scratched it from the list and were left with nine provinces left.

From the remaining nine, we didn't have any preferences between them, as our main goal was to select the one where we would have the better chances at being successful. Based on that, we decided to filter them depending on the unemployment rate, median salaries in our professions, and available opportunities. By doing this, from nine provinces we narrowed it down to three, based on the fact that these three provinces were the ones with the best job markets within Canada. These three were British Columbia, Alberta, and Ontario. Within each province, we also selected the city where we would like to move to, and these were Vancouver, Calgary and Toronto.

The top one in our list was Toronto, due to the fact that this province is just one nonstop five hour long flight away from the Dominican Republic, which meant that our family would be able to visit us without much hassle. It also has a big Dominican community, although that didn't affect our selection process, as one of our goals when moving to Canada was to integrate with the Canadian population, instead of trying to continue living in a little Dominican Republic within Canada, but still, having access to the culture of your place of origin is always a plus.

Second in our list was Vancouver, mainly because of the mild weather compared to the rest of the country. With us coming from a tropical island in the Caribbean, a place like Vancouver was appealing to us as the winters would be shorter and less harsh. It's also a world renown city, which means that many of the people we love would want to visit. On the downside, travelling to and from the Dominican Republic is a long and extenuating ordeal, as there are no direct flights on that route.

On third place was Calgary. This city is big enough, but unlike Toronto or Vancouver, it's not a well-known place. Until I started studying Canada, I didn't even know this city existed. What we liked about it was the fact that it was in the middle of nowhere, which meant that the city had vast areas to expand to and continue its growth, and implied the need for building the infrastructure required in the surrounding areas to support that growth. All of that translated in opportunities in the construction industry, our area of expertise.

So, with three cities pre-selected, we needed to pick one of the three for it to become our new home and the place where we would raise our family and grow professionally. Next, we tried to be objective about our goals, and made a list of all pros and cons of living on each one of the three cities. To do that, we needed to go to the granular level on day-to-day things, like schooling, public transport, healthcare, etc. Once we dove into that, all of the sudden Calgary started to look like the better option. It had less crime than the other two contenders, which was a big plus. Housing was also a lot cheaper in Calgary, especially when compared to Vancouver. This one thing ultimately got Vancouver dropped from the list, as we didn't want to move to a place where owning a house was impossible unless you were rich. With only Toronto and Calgary to choose from, as much as we liked Toronto, we decided to pick Calgary as the winner, due to the fact that job opportunities in Calgary were in much bigger quantities, with similar pay range, yet with far less competition. The lower cost of living also helped the balance incline towards Calgary. Finally, we had a place to hopefully call home in the near future.

With our province and city selected, the next step was to look at schools for our kids, as the school we chose would command where we lived within the city. We wanted a public school, as we were not very fond of private schooling, and with Canada having a top-notch public schooling system, there wasn't a need for us to even think about private schooling. We also wanted a school where our kids, who knew no English at all and only spoke Spanish, could get the help they needed in order to learn and transition into the English language while still getting the education they needed. Luckily for us, there are public schools with foreign language immersion programs in many cities throughout Canada, with the Spanish immersion program being one of them. After reading and investigating, we found out several schools we could choose from, so all that was left for us was to pick one that was in an area where we liked (schools in Canada depend on the neighbourhood you live in). We then investigated which were the best places to live at in Calgary, taking into consideration crime rates, school system rating, and cost of housing, among others, and based on that we finally chose a specific neighbourhood, and its related Spanish immersion public school. With the neighbourhood and school selected, we then proceeded to learn the steps of how to enroll our kids in that specific school, so that when we arrived we knew exactly where to go and avoid wasting time. We didn't hesitate in contacting the school and asking questions, and by doing that we got valuable advice that helped us find the information we needed.

We now had selected not just the province where we were moving to, but also the city, the neighbourhood, and even the school where our kids would go to. Once we were finally approved, and had a date for leaving our birth country, we started looking for a house to rent, but by this time we already knew everything we needed to know about the neighbourhood we wanted to live at, so it was quite easy for us to know when we saw a good deal, and what a good location was. We were lucky enough to find a house in a nice cul-de-sac, just one block away from the school we wanted for our kids, and the owners of the house turned out to be really nice people that were trustworthy enough to believe in us and decided to rent us the house despite us not having any references in Canada. I'm happy to say that it turned out to be a great place to live at, and we even became friends with the owners of the house.

See how many things we needed to take into account and juggle with when preparing ahead and choosing where to live at? That's exactly what you need to do, get down to the little details in order to make all of the choices you need to make and avoid leaving anything up in the air. Whether you do it like this or not will have a major effect on the start of your new life once you arrive to your new country, and the more prepared you arrive, the less surprises you'll encounter and the easier it will be for you and your accompanying family to adapt to your new environment.

CHAPTER 9

Don't Be Afraid and
Follow Through

Fear of the unknown is part of human nature, and it will surely play a big part on this journey during the initial months after you emigrate. You should be prepared for this, so that when the second thoughts start coming, you are able to push them away and continue plowing through.

Have you ever heard anyone talking about taking a leap of faith? Well, that phrase couldn't be more well suited for the subject that we are addressing in this book. As much as you do your homework and due diligence into meticulously investigating and studying about everything related to the country that you want to emigrate to, there will always be a level of uncertainty, and there's no way for you to know for sure how all of this will play out at the end.

Will you be able to adapt to your new country? Will you be able to succeed professionally? Will you be able to properly integrate into that new society? Will you get homesick, feel lonely, or want to come back to where you came from? Will you run into any unforeseen events for which you don't have a plan to address? These are just a few examples of the many, many questions that you just can't answer with a fair share of certainty. The only thing that you can know for sure is that you will not be sure of anything. All of the work you've done to prepare yourself for this new endeavour will not guarantee that you will succeed in achieving each and every single one of your goals, but what all of that hard work can do is to get you as prepared as possible for what's about to come, and give you the best chances you could have for success on this venture.

The one thing you can count on is the fact that you won't know unless you try. In my books, it's best to fail trying than not trying at all. Just imagine all of the good things you might be missing out if you are finally approved for emigrating to a place you like and where you believe you could have lots of opportunities that you don't have access to in the place you currently live at, and then you decide not to follow through with your plan and just give up. You wouldn't be able to know for sure whether or not you would have grown exponentially in your career, or how much your work-life balance would have improved, or how many new people would have become your friends, or how your overall quality of life would have changed. There's just so much for you to miss out on if you let your fear for the unknown overpower you and decide to quit and lose this incredible opportunity. Remember, you can always go back if you end up in a situation where you are no longer happy, so there's really nothing to lose by giving yourself the chance to try something new that has so much potential for improving your life in so many different ways.

Having fear is perfectly normal. Fear of the unknown is just your consciousness doing a self-check to confirm that you are aware of all the potential threats surrounding a specific decision or situation, and that you are as prepared as possible to confront them. So you shouldn't be scare of fear, in fact, you should embrace it, as it will help you make the best and more sound decisions you can make. If anyone tells you that they've never experienced fear or doubt when making such an important decision as moving abroad, I believe those people are not giving you an honest response.

Someone who is willing to leave everything behind and start over from scratch will always have fear of what's about to come, it's just human nature. What's really important is what you do with that fear. You can gain a lot by having fear, if you know how to use it to your advantage. If instead of letting that fear dictate your approach and prevent you from trying new and different things, you use it to be more careful and prepared about each of the steps you need to take when trying something different, then you will have a higher chance of success when you give it a shot. So don't be afraid of fear, but exploit it instead.

You also need to believe in yourself, and trust that the reasons you've come up with at the very beginning of this journey are valid enough for you to risk whatever it is that fear is telling you not to risk. You need to believe in the plan you've created, acknowledging that you've put a lot of thought, time and effort into it, and that there shouldn't be any reason why that plan would fail. Believe that the risk of it failing is smaller than the reality that awaits you at your current location should you decide to quit without trying.

In my case, there wasn't a single day where I wasn't afraid or worried about what was coming my way, especially once I found out that I was accepted. I remember that day, when I saw that my credit card had been billed for the initial immigration fees, I was ecstatic at the beginning, happy as a clam that all of my effort had come to fruition and that the hope for a better life was on the right path into becoming a reality, but then, after a while, that extreme happiness started to turn into worry, and by the end of the day, my head felt ten pounds heavier due to all the crazy things that came to my mind.

The next several days I couldn't even sleep, just thinking about all that I would be risking by going ahead with my plan, and about all the potential things that could go wrong once there. What got me through the doubts was the well-built plan I had already made, supported by a very solid set of reasons why to move abroad, so as much as my mind was trying to make me change course, whenever I reviewed my plan and its reasons, the doubts and hesitation were squashed, as the logic behind my decision was so powerful, that the crazy thoughts were immediately shut down.

What I'm trying to get to, is that you need to trust in yourself and your instinct, and continue moving forward until the end no matter how many tricks your mind tries to play on you. Don't be afraid of the unknown, and instead be excited by the adventure that is coming ahead, as in most cases, following through with your plan will pay off, like it did on my case.

CHAPTER 10

Be Ready to Downgrade

To increase your chances of success, you may need to lower your expectations and be ready to downgrade, both your standard of living as well as your professional status during the first stages of your new life, knowing that in time, with hard work you should be able to eventually level up and even surpass those standards.

A long the years since I emigrated, people have approached me many times for advice with regards to emigrating to Canada, the country of my choosing. As I previously said some chapters back in this book, most of them have been Dreamers, people that want to make themselves or others believe they want to emigrate, but that in reality, they truly don't want that to ever happen. Among that group, one thing that stroke me as odd was the fact that several of them found that the level of income and standard of living that I had in Canada were not high enough compared to their standards or compared to what they would expect to have if they ended up moving here.

Remember, we are talking about people living in a developing country filled with crime, poverty and corruption, comparing their standard of living with the one I had in a developed country with one of the highest standards of living in the planet. They found that the potential salary they could expect at the beginning of their arrival was subpar with what they would expect to earn based on their education and their current professional status. The time lapse that usually passes since you arrive to your new country until you get a job related to your area of expertise wasn't amusing to them either, as they believed that their qualifications were so good that Canada would be waiting for them with their dream job as soon as they landed at the airport. The possibility of starting at a lower or different position than the one they left back home wasn't something that they would even entertain. They also felt that every-day things that most people in the developed world do by themselves around their house, like fixing a plugged toilet, cutting the grass, shoveling snow, washing the dishes, or something as mundane as brooming the floor, were beneath their status and almost felt insulted about the idea of them having to do some of those activities.

They never bothered to do the numbers and realize that with a lower salary in Canada you could do a lot more than with the bigger salary they were supposedly earning back home, as the cost of living in Canada was far less than the one in Dominican Republic (surprising, but true). Healthcare in Canada is free, something that is not the case in the Dominican Republic, so just there you have a lot of potential savings in the event you are in need of medical care. But since most healthy people don't care about that kind of thing until they or one of their loved ones fall in sick, the free healthcare is a mute point for them. Public schooling is also free in Canada, and it's of top quality. As previously explained, my kids were enrolled in a bilingual (English – Spanish) school, and I didn't have to pay a dime. Back home, the public school system is of the lowest quality you can imagine, and in order for kids to have a chance of a better future in the grownup world, they need to go to a private school, all of them with prices up the roof, and I'm not even talking about the bilingual ones, as the cost for those is prohibitive, only reserved for the rich. Food is also cheaper in Canada, same as gas, cars, utilities, etc. The only thing more expensive in Canada than back home is housing, and even so, mortgage rates are so low, that it's still 100 times easier to buy a house in Canada than in the Dominican Republic. Nevertheless, these things didn't seem to matter to the people I'm referring to.

Same thing happens with the chores I mentioned earlier. With the Dominican Republic being so poor, people in the middle class or above can afford having a maid to do all the work around the house. Cutting grass was for their gardener, and for unplugging a toilet, most of them would just call a plumber who would charge them pennies for his/her time. So, all of these perks were hard for them to let go and accept that once they moved abroad, they would have to do all of these tasks themselves. They'd rather stay back home than even think about the possibility of them doing such activities.

One thing you need to be clear about is that no country is giving you stuff for free and without hard work. If you move to another country, you are starting there from scratch, just like everyone else in that country did before you and will continue to do after you. If you truly want to move abroad, you have to be flexible and willing to do everything you need to do in order to make it, and if that means doing your own housekeeping, or doing the same work your gardener did for you back in your home country then that's what you need to do. You also need to understand that the new country you are going to, despite the fact that they want you there to enrich their population with your culture and knowledge, is also not desperate to have you, as there are millions more just like you, that are doing the same process you are doing. As much as they want you there, they won't be waiting for you at the airport with your dream job. You have to realize that you need to do your work, putting time and effort into looking and applying for jobs, and acknowledge that there's a big possibility that you'll need to start at a lower position than the one you had back home, and accept the fact that doing that is perfectly Ok. Chances are that you'll still have a better financial situation in a lower position at your new country, than the one you had back home with a higher position, and even if that's not the case, you need to remember that you are starting from scratch at this new place, without any work references, so if getting into a lesser position is what gets you introduced into the labour market, then that's what you need to do, knowing that with your hard work and experience you will most likely advance in your career at giant leaps. Also, you need to accept that getting a job in your area of expertise is not a couple of days kind of thing. You will need to apply to dozens, and maybe even hundreds of jobs before you land one, and that could take several months, and in some cases even close to a year, and this is something you need to be aware of from the get-go in order not to despair and lose hope. You might even have to start in an industry not related at all to what you used to do before, just to get the bills paid, while you continue your search for something that falls within your previous expertise, and that's Ok. Being flexible and open to change is what will help you succeed at the end.

In my case, I took me six months and more than three hundred resumes (yes, you read correctly, three hundred), to finally get a job in the construction industry in a field related to what I used to do back home. It was a lesser position, and somewhat different to what I had previously done in my professional life, but it was something that I could relate to, and which I could learn from. The salary was enough for me and my family to make a living without any shortcomings, and the position allowed me to meet people and make new connections that helped me grow within the company, and to eventually jump ships to another company where I was hired as Project Manager, the same position I had when I left my country of birth, and with a better salary, all of that in just 3 years. I mow the lawn every two weeks in the summer, shovel the snow every snowy day during winter, clean the kitchen every day after dinner, and unplug the toilets when needed (which surprisingly, for some weird reason it happens way too often at my house), and I do all of that with a smile on my face. Had I had the same mentality as the people described at the beginning of this chapter, I would still be living in the Dominican Republic, most likely struggling to make ends meet, and if not, living the dream in Paradise, locked in a cage protecting me from the outside, living in my own cell as a trusted inmate.

CHAPTER 11

Once There, Search For All Available Help

As a new immigrant, you'll need to tap into all the help that you can find to successfully insert yourself into your new society. Finding this help will be your responsibility, and looking for it should be your main task during the early phase of your move abroad.

Kudos to you! Once you are at this stage, it means that you've been approved to emigrate, and by now you have either emigrated, or are planning on a set date to emigrate. You think you are out of the woods, and that all the nasty work is already done. Well, you are wrong my friend. Getting there was just half the battle, now the real hard work begins in order for you to insert yourself into the new society that you've chosen and become one of its productive members.

Depending on where you emigrate to, there may be programs in place which have been tailored specifically to help newcomers transition into their new society. You need to do your due diligence to find out which programs these are, and to see whether or not you meet the requirements to apply for those. Search online, go to forums, visit an immigration centre, call a government information office, ask other immigrants, or even reach out to the embassy of that country if you haven't moved there yet. Anything you can do to get all the information you need to access the programs available for new immigrants like you, you should do.

To give you a few examples, I will use my case as a reference. Please be aware that not all countries have the same tools, and with Canada being a country dependent on immigration for their success, they put a lot of effort into having as many tools as possible available for their newcomers in order to give them the best chances they can to succeed on their endeavour.

When we arrived to Canada, a social worker was assigned to me and my family to provide us with an introduction on what steps to do at the beginning, what programs we had available at our disposal to apply to, and how to start integrating. It was a lot of help having that social worker at our disposal, but we also did our own leg work by researching online. While doing that, we found information about several other programs besides the ones provided to us by the social worker. See? Had we not done our homework and only relied on the information given to us effortlessly by the social worker, we would have missed out on those other programs we found by ourselves, and some of them were pretty helpful.

Among the tools we found by investigating ourselves were courses being given only to newcomers to adapt them to the labour market of Canada, and to bridge them into a job. There were programs where we could access free dental care, free eye care and free medications (medications are not expensive in Canada, but they are not free). There was also guidance on where to get free help with daily living activities, like accounting and legal services, or where to apply and get a credit card without having any credit history in Canada.

So, as you can see, it is pretty important that you don't rely solely in the information given to you by one person or institution, and you should search for additional data by other means and in different places, as there may be guidance available somewhere else that the person or institution helping you is not fully aware of.

Also, don't be shy of using all help available. If it's there for you to use, it's because you are entitled to it, and you have the right to access it when you want or when you need it. I remember that as newcomers, we had access to free groceries about seven times a year. Since we were not poor or homeless, we could choose not to use it, and buy food with our savings, but we had no idea how long it would take for us to get a job, and we had no monetary income whatsoever, so we decided to get the free groceries during that first year only. We were hesitant at the beginning, because we believed only poor people should use this aid, but we decided it was best for us to access this service in order to stretch our savings as much as possible in case getting a job took longer than expected. I'm glad we did, not only because it helped us keep our peace of mind by not having to spend that money when we had no jobs, but it also opened up our eyes to see how much these programs help the less fortunate, and how grateful people are when they see others helping them. Once we got jobs, we started donating food regularly to the food bank as a way of paying back for the help they provided us when we needed it.

Bottom line, don't just leave it to others to explain how to access aid and support. Do you own research in a detailed and thorough way, and don't stop until you believe you've found all existing information about programs designed to help you start your new life in your new country. Lastly, never feel ashamed of using any of the available support at your disposal. The whole point of the existence of these programs is precisely for people like you to use them and to benefit from them. In a situation like the one you've embarked yourself on, the   more   help   you   can   get,   the   better.

CHAPTER 12

Start Networking

Meeting other people, especially within your profession, will go a long way towards helping place yourself into the job market, and into society.

Along with all the help and support that you should search for and apply to as soon as you arrive at your new destination, as explained on the previous chapter, another important activity you should also focus your attention on is networking. "What is networking?", you may ask. Well, networking means interacting with other people with the intention of expanding your professional and social contacts. In your case, this is of extreme importance for two reasons. First, you want to start getting to know people around you to try to get your social life going in your new country. As social beings that we are, interacting with people in a social way is of great importance, and it will help you adapt faster and easier to your new society. Second, you need to start creating a professional base that can help you insert yourself into the labour market. This last one is of special relevance, as in most societies the chances of getting hired in your area of expertise are highly increased by meeting people, especially from within your same industry, and interfacing with them. To say it in other words, you have better chances of landing a job by networking, than by applying to jobs online. By this I'm not saying that you will not be able to get a job solely by online methods, as in my case that's exactly how I got my first job in Canada, but with networking you have better odds of getting a job faster than if you only applied online.

Contrary to what you may believe, even in highly advanced societies, personal connections and who you know do matter. Recommendations from people within the community give you a great advantage when trying to get a job, and the advantage is even greater when the recommendation comes from a professional colleague with contacts within your own profession. There are many jobs available out there that are not even being posted online, and those positions are being filled by the companies with people that their employees know and have referred to. As such, the more people you get to know, and the more connections you make, the better.

In the social realm, getting to know people that share your same values is always important, and even more when those people live close by to where you live. For the most part, people are usually interested in meeting new folks, especially when they come from different places with different cultures. Approaching your neighbours is a great way to start meeting people, as everybody wants to know who's the new guy who moved next door. You will notice that most of them will be quite interested in your story, and some of them will most likely try to help giving you advice on how to adapt to your new environment, how to meet more people, or even tips on how to land a job. If you are a shy person, you should put your shy suit aside, put your courage pants on, and make an effort to get out of your comfort zone and start making conversation with people around you. I met one of my best friends in Canada by just talking to him every morning when I took the kids to school. Every day we talked a bit more, and eventually I invited him to my house to meet my family, and pretty soon we were visiting each other and without even planning for it, we became very good friends. Same with my neighbours, when we moved there, we visited each one of them with a bag of cookies to introduce ourselves, and by doing that we became part of that community right from the get-go, and even though we eventually moved to another neighbourhood, we have kept closely in touch with many of them. The relationships created are so honest and real, that I know without a doubt that if I ever need a hand from them in a time of need, they will help me without hesitation. Knowing that you have people like that where you live, people that you can count on, is priceless, and you can only get that by getting the ball rolling, introducing yourself to as much people as you can, and continuously nurturing those relationships you create with them.

With regards to the professional circle that you should aim to create, you should search online for forums or conferences related your profession and attend those. You should also check if there is a professional association related to your career that you could join, and if so, you should attend any meetings or seminars that they plan. These are excellent places to meet people from your profession or related industry, while at the same time you can get a lot of value from these events. Another way you can meet other professionals is by searching for professional networks, as in many cities there are networks that have been created with the sole purpose of helping people get to know others from their same profession. It is not uncommon to invite someone for a cup of coffee to chat about your career, and many people will do their best to provide you with information that can help you get to where you want to get. Once you land a job, your professional network will continue to grow, but this time at an exponential rate, and should you choose to switch jobs in the future, it will help you achieve this much more easily and with less effort than when you first started creating it.

In conclusion, networking will help you in more ways than you can think of, so you should put a lot of effort on this activity, making sure you take all the opportunities that come your way to create, grow and maintain both your social and professional networks. Once you do that, you'll be able to eventually reap the benefits in a wide variety of situations. So, what are you waiting for? Get your butt off that couch and start networking!

CHAPTER 13

Integrate

Integrating to your new society is the best way for you to become part of the country that has accepted you as one of their own, and will provide you with different opportunities to benefit from.

When you integrate, you bring two or more things together to create a whole and act as one. That is the final goal that every emigrant should aim for. As a new member of a society that has been kind and generous enough to open its doors for you with the intention of having you become a productive member of the community while at the same time being free to exploit and enjoy all of the benefits that come along with being part of it, it is your moral obligation to put all the necessary effort into absorbing that new culture and becoming one of them.

It is very common to see immigrants clustered into groups of people that come from their same native country, and while there's nothing wrong with finding and staying close to other immigrants from your birthplace that are experiencing or have experienced the same situation that you are, it's another thing to have your social life become exclusive or mostly exclusive to them. Remember, you are the one who chose to move out of your country of birth and into the new country that accepted you and allowed you to become one of them, so instead of trying to convert your surroundings into a copy of your place of origin, you should focus on making an effort to study and understand the culture of this new society that has received you, and try to take in as much of that culture as you can. In other words, you need to integrate.

Going back to my own emigration experience, when we moved to Canada, many people wanted us to move to Toronto, mainly because in that city there's a big Dominican community. That fact never was taken into account by us when deciding which city to emigrate to, as from the early conception of the idea of moving abroad, it was our intention to fully integrate with our new society and become one more of the group. Doing that not only enriched our overall knowledge about the country of our choosing, but it also helped us improve as human beings, as we were absorbing new and different perspectives of life and ways of thinking that we had no access to at our place of birth. Had we chosen to stay clustered with only other Dominicans instead, we would have missed out on many cultural advantages that our new society had to offer.

Not only that, but the people of your new country do notice when you want to become one of them, and when you'd rather stay living in a bubble of your former homeland within your new country, and I can assure you that the latter group is often ignored when opportunities arise. Just think of it this way, if a neighbour moved next door to you, and didn't make an effort to get to know you, or to learn what's your story, what your values are, or anything that relates to you, would you want to offer your support to that person? I'm pretty sure your answer is no. People rather engage with and provide support to individuals that show interest in them and in their culture, and to the ones who make an effort to learn about their new society and to become one more of the pack. The ones that distance themselves from integrating to their new society are sometimes ignored by the community, and when opportunities arise, these people are often not considered to have them benefit from those.

In Calgary, the place we chose to live at, while overall it's a pretty heterogenous community, there are whole sections of the city populated mostly by people from the same ethnicity and culture. In my eyes, as an immigrant myself, I believe that's a mistake, as new immigrants should try to blend in with the general population of their new country, and you can only get that by diluting yourself among them, not by segregating yourself and sticking together with others from your birthplace. Had the immigrants that live in those communities chosen to integrate with the Canadian population instead of clustering in bubbles that resemble their native land, I'm sure their emigration experience would have been far better and more enriching than what it has most likely been. Moreover, by keeping themselves away from people that are native to the country that they have emigrated to, they are denying the general population from the ability to learn and expand their knowledge about other cultures, preventing their own values and customs from expanding into their new country.

This last sentence I just wrote is quite important. Integration is not just a one-way street, it's actually a two-way street, which means that newcomers, besides taking in their host country's culture, they also need to share their own culture with the people of their new community. Doing that will only improve the general culture of your new homeland, making it richer and more interesting. So, as much as you need to integrate by blending in and absorbing the culture of your new society, you should also aim to keep and embrace your own culture, as that is part of what defines you. Most individuals from your new country will be interested in knowing about other places and about their culture, so you should exploit that interest and use it for expanding the overall knowledge of your new community with regards to your place of birth.

Lastly, you shouldn't confuse integration with assimilation. These are two completely different words that mean very different things. When moving abroad, you want to integrate to your new society in order to become one of them, but you should not want to assimilate that society's values and culture by suppressing your own. There's good and bad in every society, and your ultimate goal as an immigrant should be to absorb the good things about your new culture, making sure you keep away the bad things that also come along, and at the same time keeping the good things from the culture of your place of birth, and letting go of the bad things it also has. As previously stated, if you do that, you will only help making your new country a place with a richer culture, more accepting, and more inclusive.

CHAPTER 14

Be Patient

You must accept the fact that things will not always happen when or how you want them to happen. You need to soak up yourself with patience and prepare your mindset to adjust to the unforeseen and to learn to change and adapt accordingly.

They say that patience is a virtue, and I couldn't agree more. But (yes, there's always a but), on the scenario that we are discussing in this book, patience is not a virtue, it's a MUST. Acknowledging that you will have to face situations where things don't go according to your plans is critical for your success on this journey, both during the application process, but especially once you have moved abroad. I use the word "especially" in the latter case, because it is one thing to lose patience during the application process and end up giving up while you are still in your country of origin, and it's another thing to lose patience after you've emigrated, just to end up quitting and turning back just because you didn't have the fortitude to cope with the fact that things were not happening when you believed they should, or how you were expecting them to happen.

As in any project that you work on, whether it's a project from work, or like in this case, a personal life changing project, you need to recognize that there will be risks, and after identifying them, you need to prepare a plan in order to deal with them if and when they arise. You can't just cowboy your way into your new life without any contingency plan for the potential issues that can and will present in front of you, you have to be prepared. You also need to understand that, for as much as you've analyzed all potential risks, there will be some risks that you won't be able to account for, be it due to inexperience, lack of knowledge, over expectations, or simply because these were so improbable or difficult to imagine, that you just couldn't foresee them ahead of time. These last two types of risks, the ones that were not considered due to over expectations and the ones that you simply don't know about, are the ones where being patient will do wonders for you, and where adapting to change and accepting potential alterations to your plan will be the difference between ultimately succeeding, or giving up and failing.

The most critical task you need to concentrate on when you first arrive at your new country, have settled into a home, and have done the initial paperwork to get all of your needed documentation in place, is finding a job. This activity is usually the one that provides the most stress and frustration to newcomers, as many of them emigrate believing that they will find the job of their dreams in just a few days or weeks after arriving, just to eventually realize that wasn't the case. This is a perfect example of over expectations. When emigrating, you should never over expect, always be realistic, and even under expect in some situations. Being patient on a situation like the one described, will help you continue to focus on your task without desperation or frustration, and will help you accept the fact that things will eventually fall into place if you continue to put your effort in the right place in a consistent way.

Adapting to change will also go great lengths in helping you achieve your goal eventually, albeit maybe not in the timeline you wanted to achieve it. For example, let's use once again the same searching for a dream job example. Let's suppose that you came to your new country with the expectation of getting a job doing exactly what you were doing back home, on your same profession, and earning a salary over a specific amount of money that you've placed as a minimum limit. This example, by the way, is based on a mistake, as I explained before, you should emigrate with realistic expectations, and maybe even with under expectations, ready to start at a lower position or even with a different role and lower salary than the one you had at your place of origin, but for the sake of this example, let's say that you are one of the over expecting type of people. It is definitely a possibility that you might be lucky enough and find a job that matches your criteria and with a salary that meets your parameters, in a short period of time. If that is the case, then great! You've beat the odds and are now on your way to fulfilling all of your dreams! But chances are, that's not going to be the case, and as such, you need to be ready to change and adapt yourself to that new reality. The earlier you realize that your expectations are too high, and the sooner you adapt to your new reality and change your approach and expectations, the faster you'll be able to rectify your trajectory and ultimately reach your more realistic goal.

You also need to understand that this is not a race, and that it is ok to take your time to get to where you want to get. When I arrived to Canada, it took me six months to land my first job. As a Civil Engineer, I wanted to find a job in the construction industry, but not necessarily as a Civil Engineer. I was clear on the fact that, in Canada, I wasn't considered a Civil Engineer until I revalidated my education and experience, something I eventually did and which allowed me to become a certified Professional Engineer a few years later down the road. At the beginning, my title was worthless in Canada, and I was conscious of that, so I never applied for a role of Civil Engineer. Instead, I applied to roles similar to what a professional in my area would do within the construction industry, and that's how I eventually got hired. But I never thought that I was in a race against the clock to get a job with the same role as I had before emigrating. It wasn't a race for me, because my priority was to get a job and start providing for my family, whether it was in my area of expertise, or doing something entirely new or different.

In fact, at some point before getting hired, I was feeling that it was being a bit difficult for me to get into the construction industry, so I started searching for other careers unrelated to the construction industry that I could learn about and insert myself into. During that research, I noticed that there were a lot of jobs in the IT and programming industry, but since I had no knowledge at all about that, the only way for me to get into that industry was by educating myself and becoming an expert at one area of that field. Since I did some programing back when I was younger, it was something that I could relate to, and that I actually liked doing, so I searched for different programing courses, and found one that checked all of the boxes. Once I had that course selected, I then started all the paperwork needed to enroll myself into college for a two-year curriculum program to become a software programmer and start a new career, and just as I was admitted and right before I paid for my tuition, that's when I got hired. As you can see, I was ready to adapt and change, because my goal was to make it work no matter what, I wasn't married to Civil Engineering nor to the construction industry, what I wanted to do was to insert myself into the labour market and start earning money to support my family, and if a career change was what was needed, then that's what I would do.

Moving forward to when I first got hired, at that first company at the beginning I had a lesser position than the one I had before I moved to Canada, but I could relate to the duties that the role demanded, and I enjoyed doing it. In fact, I was quite good at it, so much that just in a couple of years I was promoted as manager of my department. During my time at that company, I learned a lot about the differences between the Canadian labour market compared to where I came from, as well as about the construction industry too, and it also helped me make a few friends and a lot of new professional contacts, something that eventually helped me get my second job a few years later, where I was hired as Project Manager at a construction company, doing exactly what I did back in the Dominican Republic, and earning a pretty decent salary. So, clearly, having patience worked perfectly in my case, as even though I started at a lesser position than the one I had before emigrating, I believe it was actually a blessing, and the way things happened turned out to be in my best interest, as they led to me eventually reaching the same position I originally had. Had I come to Canada with too high of expectations, and unwilling to adapt or to change, I could have run the risk of not finding a proper job and eventually failing and returning back home, where I had no future at all waiting for me.

CHAPTER 15

Be Grateful

As with everything good that happens in your life, you should be thankful and grateful for the people who helped making those good things become a reality.

Well, congratulations! Once you've reached this stage, you should be all set in your new country with a job, friends, professional contacts, and ideally enjoying the things that made you move there in the first place. This is exactly what you've worked for so hard for the last several years. Yes, you read correctly, years. Success is not built overnight, it takes lots of time and hard work, but eventually, when you get there, it's all worth it. You now live in a society that has accepted you as one of their own, you've adapted to that new environment, and hopefully you've embraced your new culture and are raising your family in a place where you feel they'll be happy and have all the necessary tools to succeed when their time comes for that.

Now, all of this would not have been possible if the country that you chose to be your new home hadn't accepted you to move there in the first place, which calls for some gratitude from your end. Not only that, but the fact that the things that make life over there so nice and worth of taking the huge risk that you took when moving there, are being given to you same as everybody else around you, is also worth appreciation and needs to be acknowledged.

Being grateful to that new society that has embraced you as one of their own is the right thing to do. "And how exactly I'm I supposed to do that?", you may ask. No, you don't have to go to a civil servant or to a police officer in the middle of the street to say "thanks for receiving me here" out of the blue. The way you say thank you is by being a well behaving citizen, by following the laws of the country you moved to, by being actively engaged in your community, by trying to help others around you when they are in need, by donating your surplus staples (like food or clothing) to the less fortunate, or by volunteering for work in your free time to help out the underprivileged, among other ways.

Your new society will appreciate those gestures, as these will only serve for the overall benefit of the general population, increasing the quality of life of everyone in the community, including you and your loved ones. I believe doing everything you can to help your new community become a better one is the best way to say thanks for the opportunities that have been given to you by them. Not only will you be showing gratitude to that nation that welcomed you, but at the same time you will feel the happiness that is only achieved when people do good deeds and help out others.

After all the opportunities that your new country has provided you with, giving back and being grateful to them is the least one can do to show appreciation for everything good that has come out of this endeavour. Now, go enjoy your new happy life as an upstanding immigrant, and make sure to always be grateful and appreciative for what you have, which, in this case, it's surely something many others want, but sadly can't have.

EPILOGUE

Rewards are things that award you for the effort you've put when doing something, or for having ideas that have translated into an improvement compared to what was previously available. I can tell you with confidence that if you follow the steps described throughout this book, chances are that you will be eventually rewarded with a positive outcome after your decision to emigrate. Just seeing your child grow in a society that shares your same values, and where there are plenty of opportunities to succeed, is a reward by itself. If you really want to emigrate and you put on all the effort that this task demands, the resulting benefits will outweigh by far all of the sacrifices that you'll need to make in order to reach your final goal.

As an emigrant myself, I am truly happy that I chose this path, and there are no words for me to describe the peace of mind and joy that I feel by watching my family grow in this new land that we now call home. I honestly hope that more people in the world are able to experience the same feelings I'm having, so my word of advice for anyone thinking that they can have a better life somewhere else other than their place of birth, is to follow that little voice of yours, and give it a try. Depending on your particular situation, chances are that there isn't much for you to lose, but there may be lots to gain. You'll be amazed at how much satisfaction can be found by proceeding with this extraordinary and exciting adventure. As the saying that I'm sure most of you have heard many times before, you'll never know until you try. So, try.

ABOUT THE AUTHOR

Born in Dominican Republic, I started thinking about the possibility of moving abroad around 2006, not long after I got married, not because I needed to do it for myself, but because I wanted to think ahead of time about the future of my yet to be born kids. After that initial thought, the desire to make that idea a reality grew little by little, until I officially initiated the emigrating process in 2011 by reading and investigating, and ultimately culminating with our acceptance into Canada and our subsequent move to Calgary, where we currently live. Just a mere 3 years after arriving we became Canadian Citizens, I got my professional credentials validated as a Professional Engineer in Alberta working as a project manager in the construction industry, and my wife had a successful daycare / art program business.

I'm devoted to helping others achieve their emigrating dreams in any way I can, as that's something that brings me joy and happiness, as well as a sense of personal fulfillment. If you have any comments, questions or concerns about anything related to emigrating, or about anything that has been discussed in this book, feel free to shoot me an email at info@smartemigrant.com and I'll do my very best at providing you with any input that I believe might be of value. Please be aware that I'm not an expert in this subject in any sense of the word, but I'm well intended and I think having someone who to approach to bounce your ideas off, or to provide you with a second opinion from a different perspective, goes a long way in this type of situation. You can also visit my website at www.smartemigrant.com where you can find some more information and tips about how to emigrate the right way. Good luck!

www.ingramcontent.com/pod-product-compliance
Lightning Source LLC
Chambersburg PA
CBHW071139280326
41935CB00010B/1297